The Fuck Off Ways

Phenomenal Swear Word To Color

For Stress Releasing

J.N. Moorcroft

Happy Coloring!

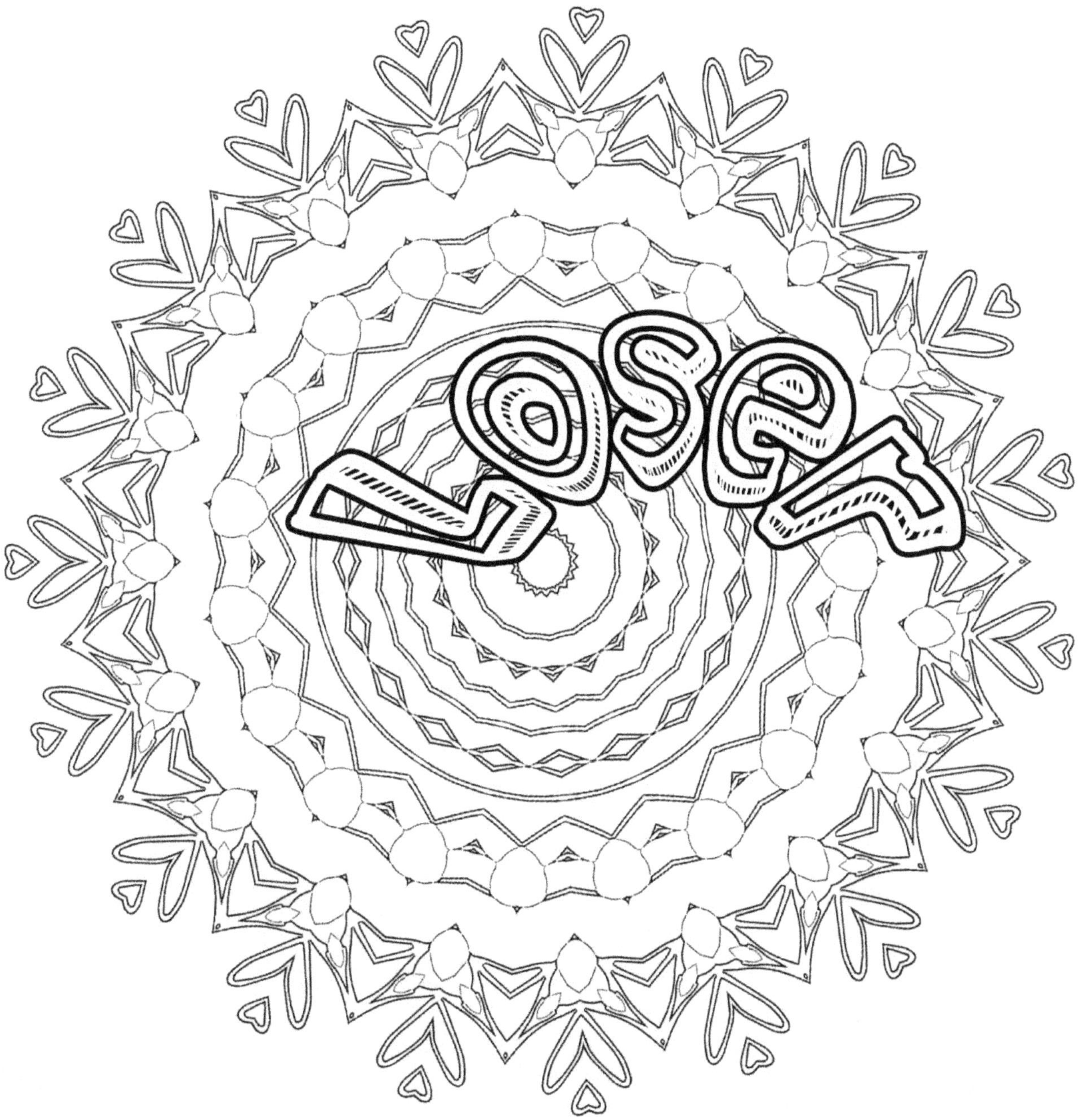
Loser

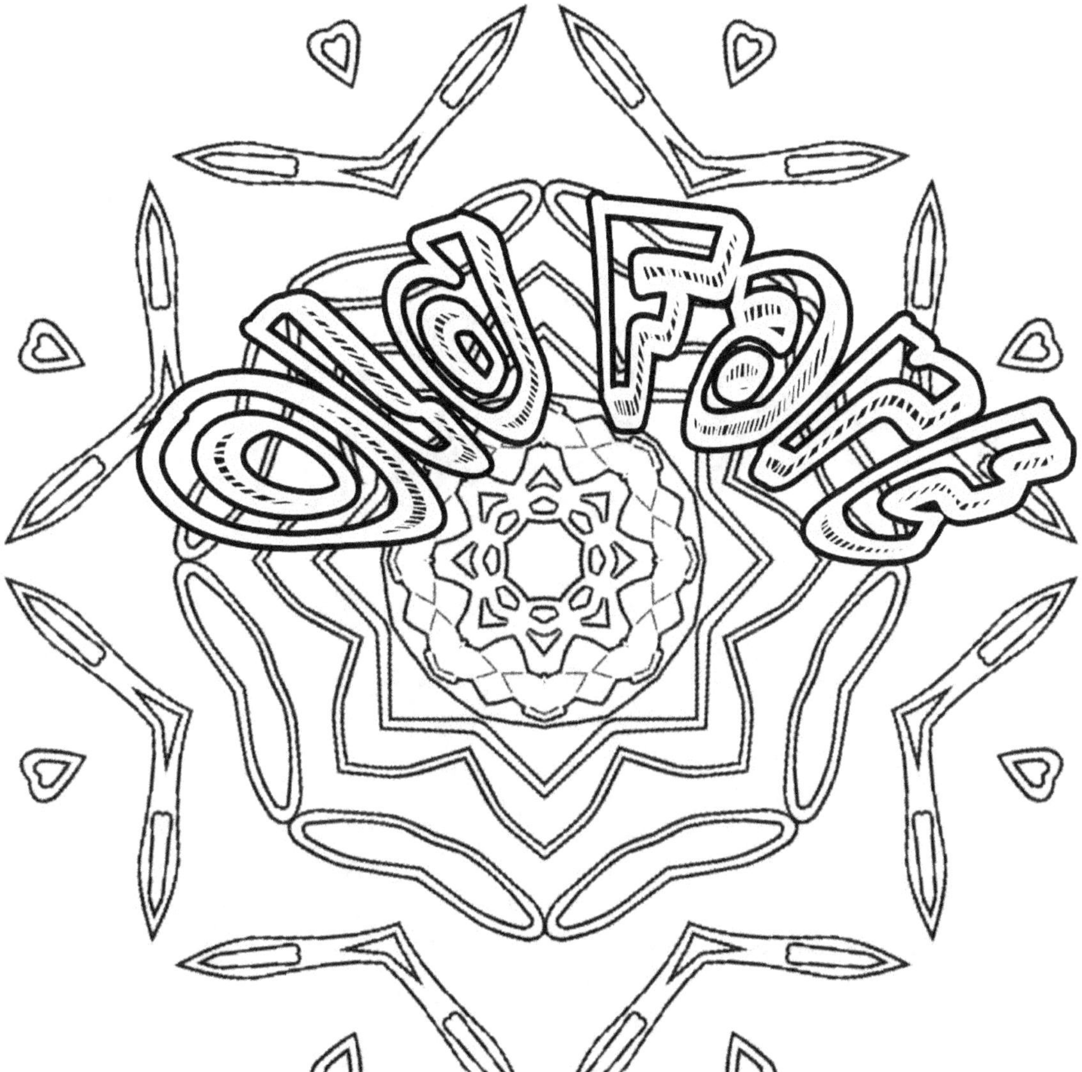
Old Fart

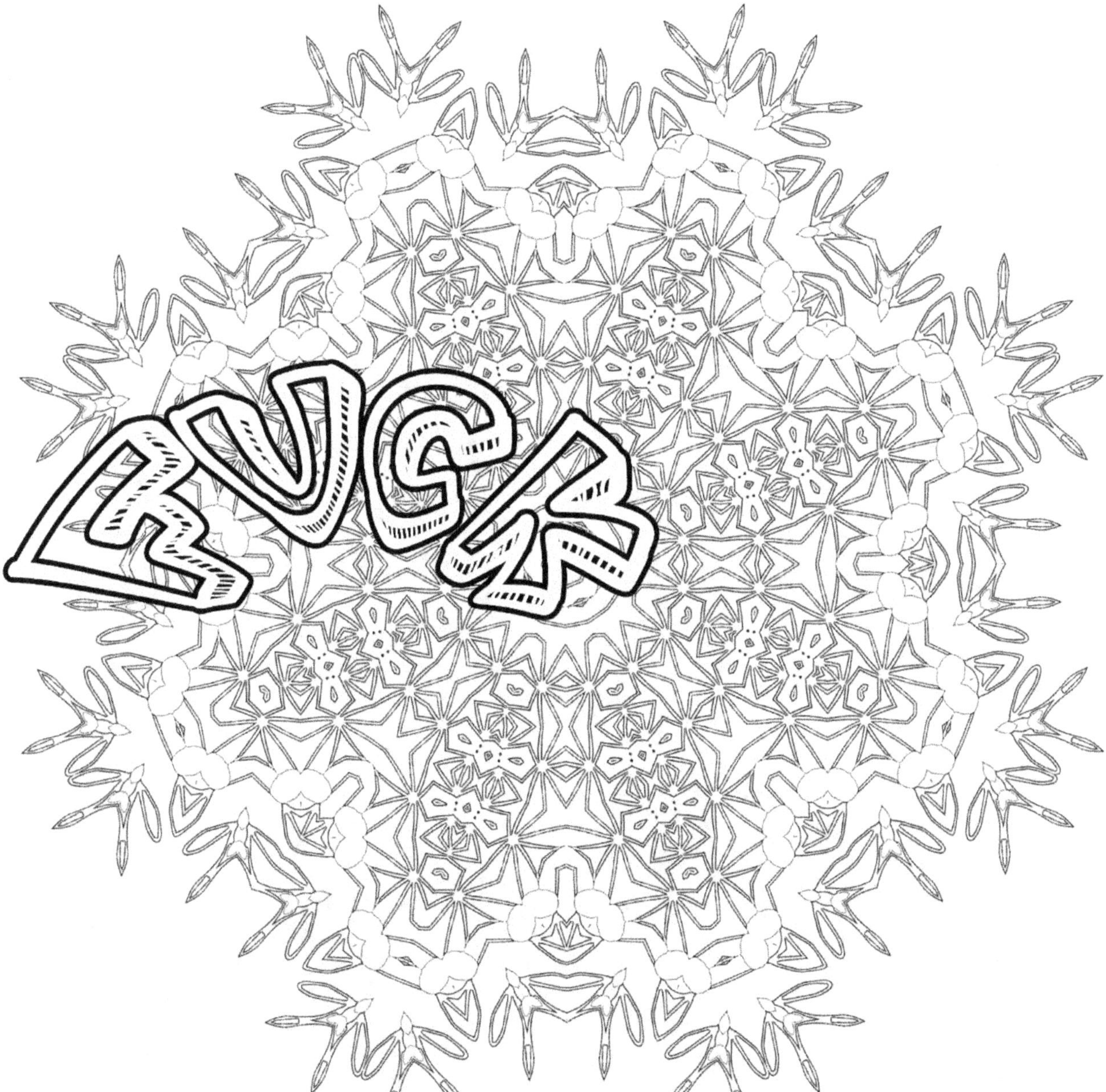

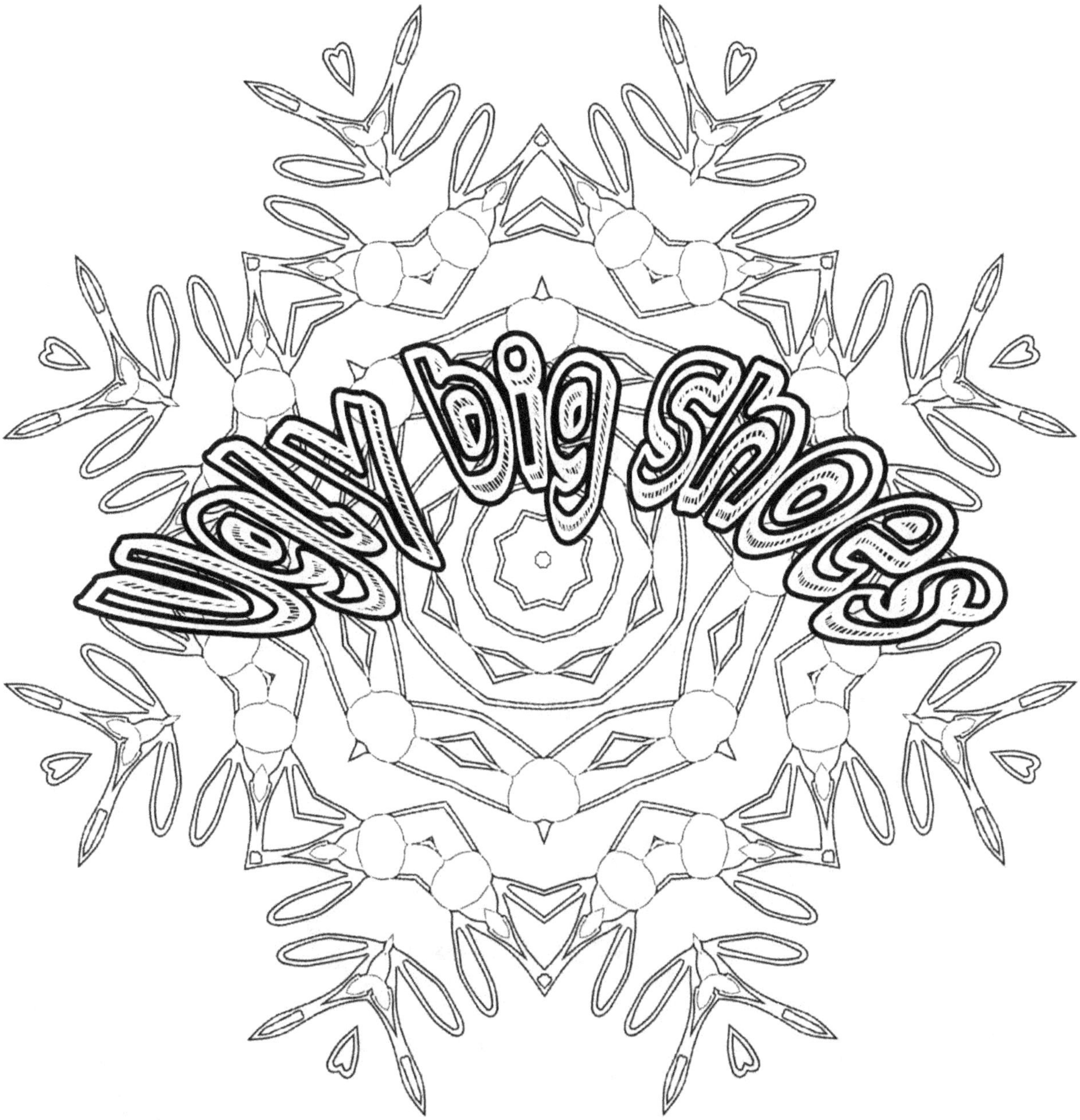
ugly big shoes

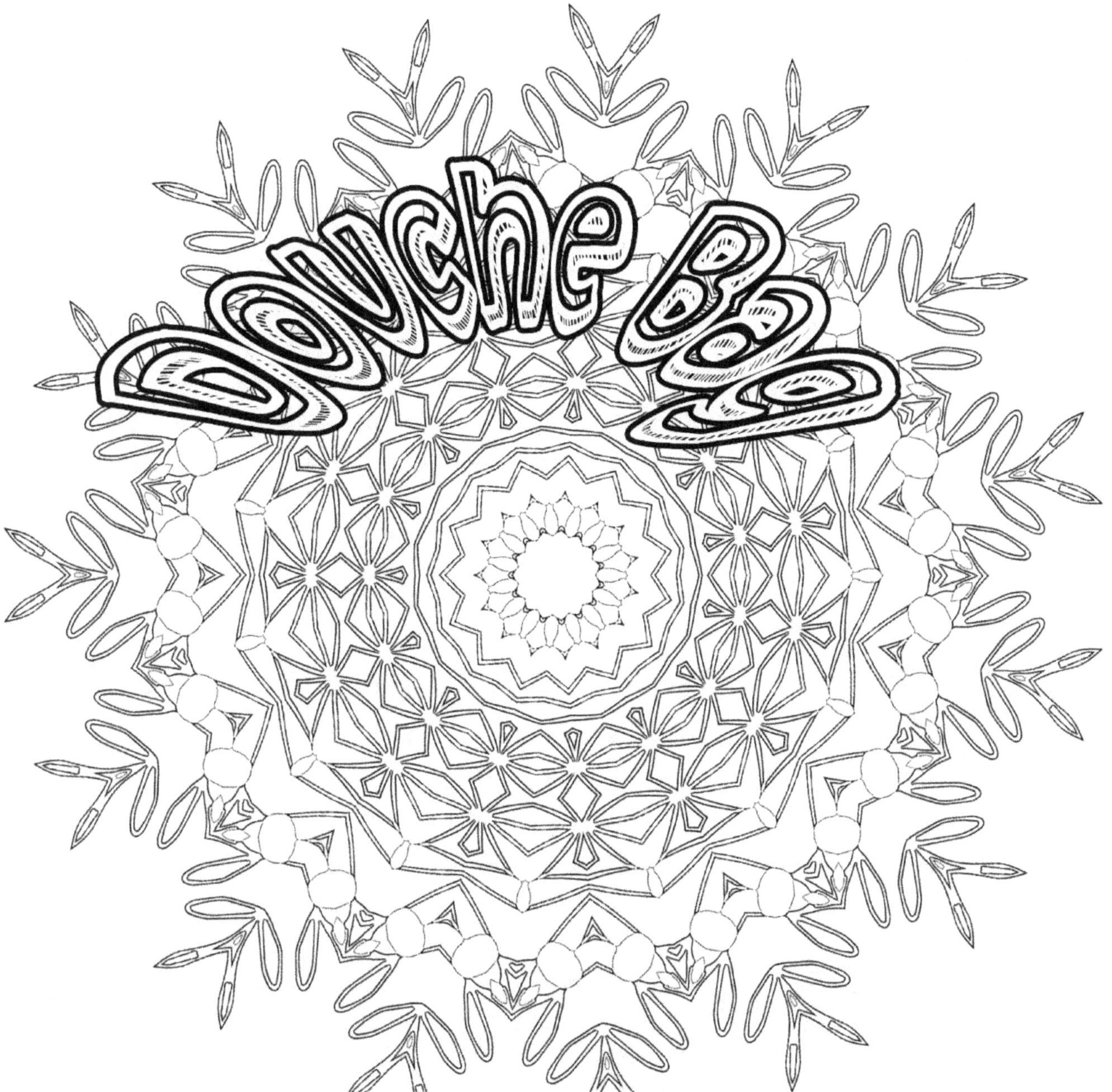
Douche Bag

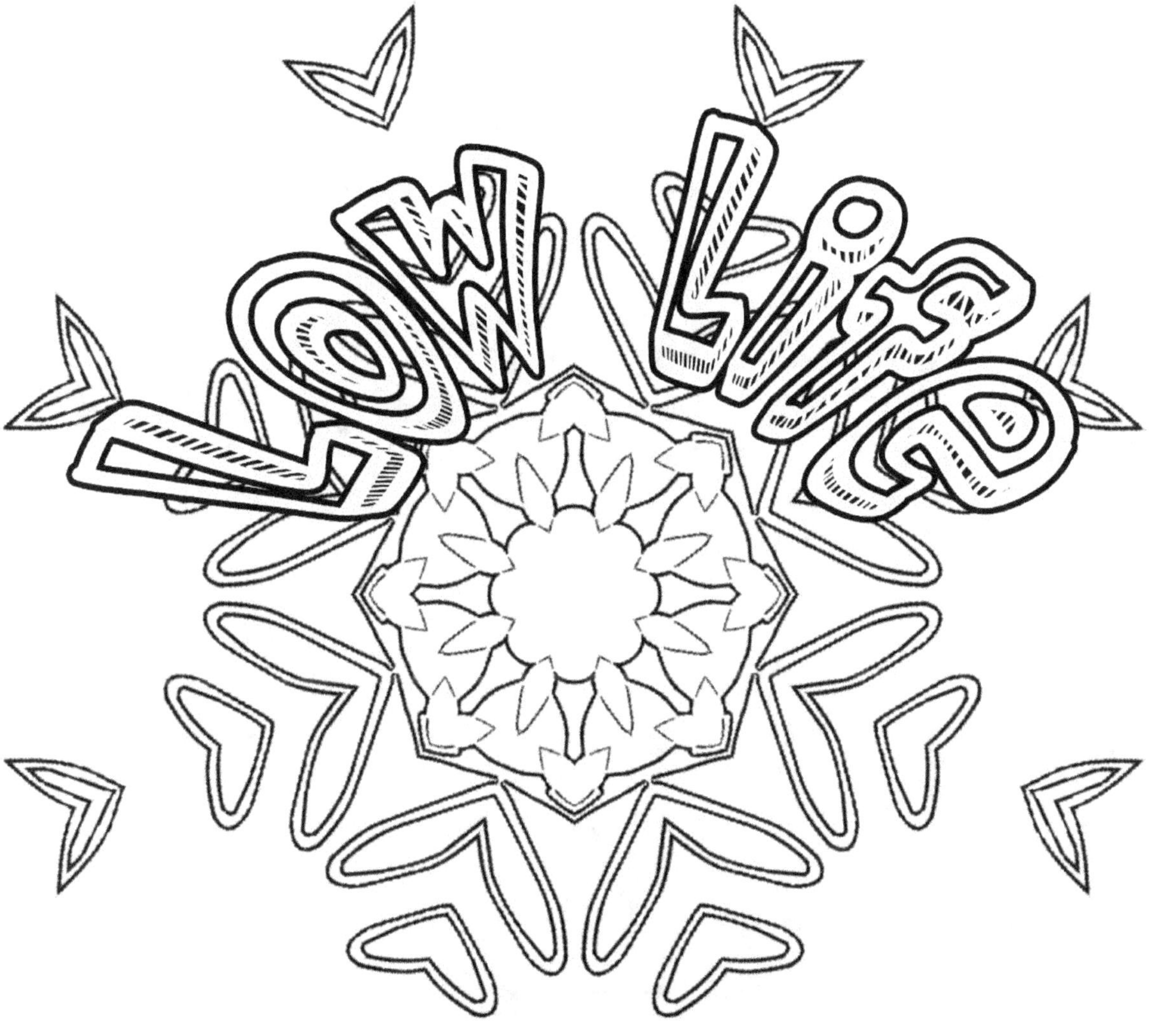
Low Life

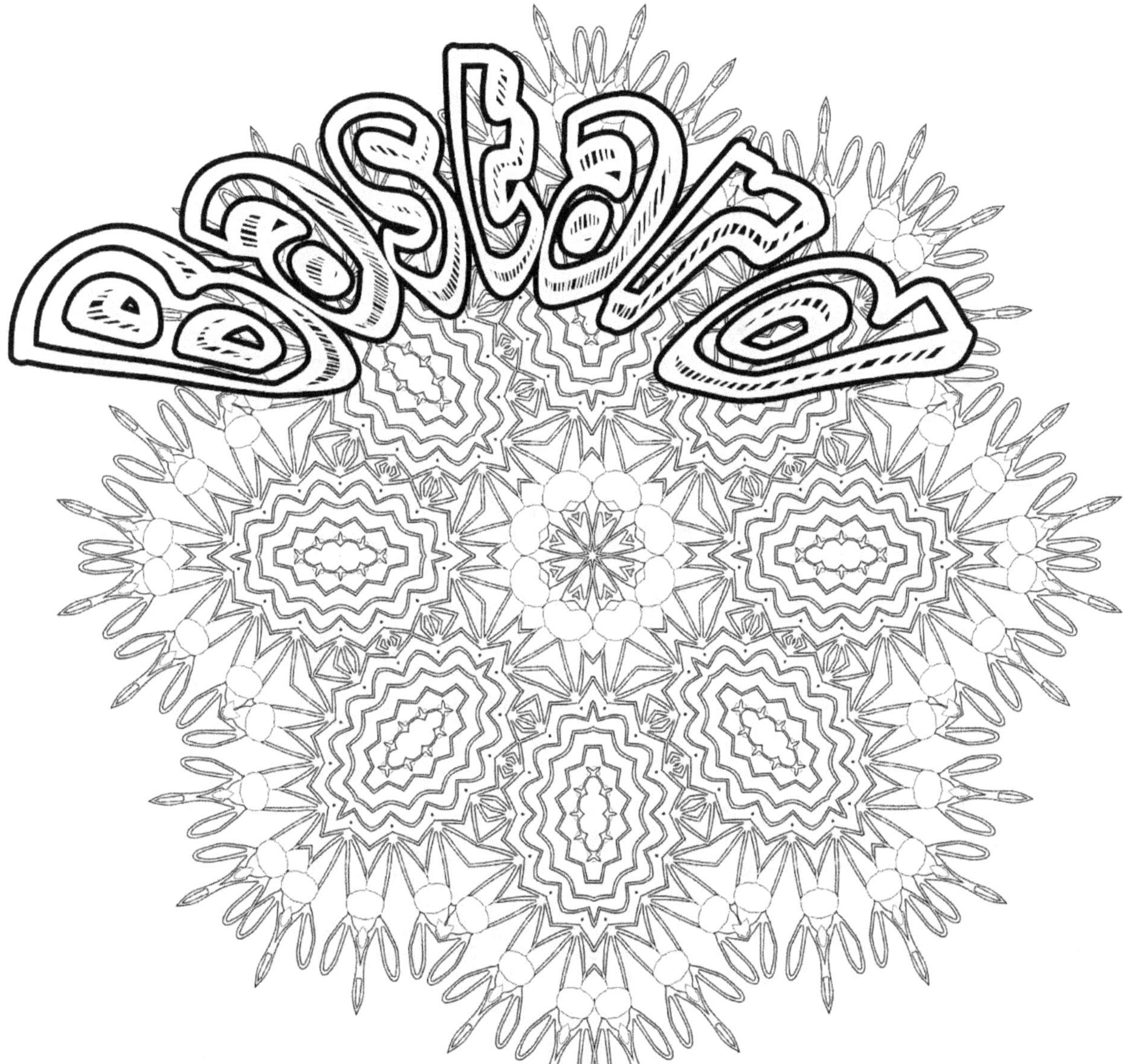
Bastard

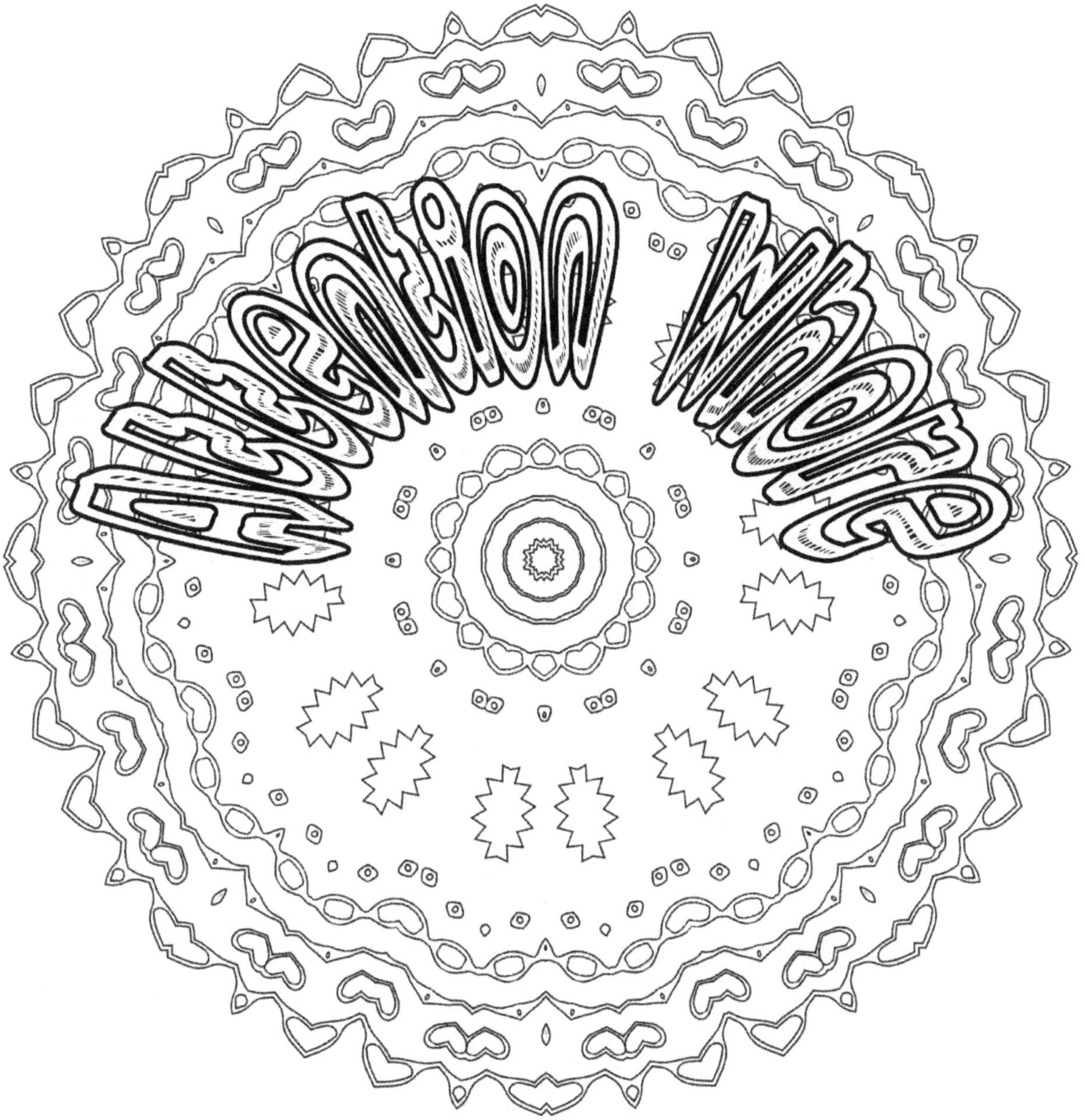
Attention Whore

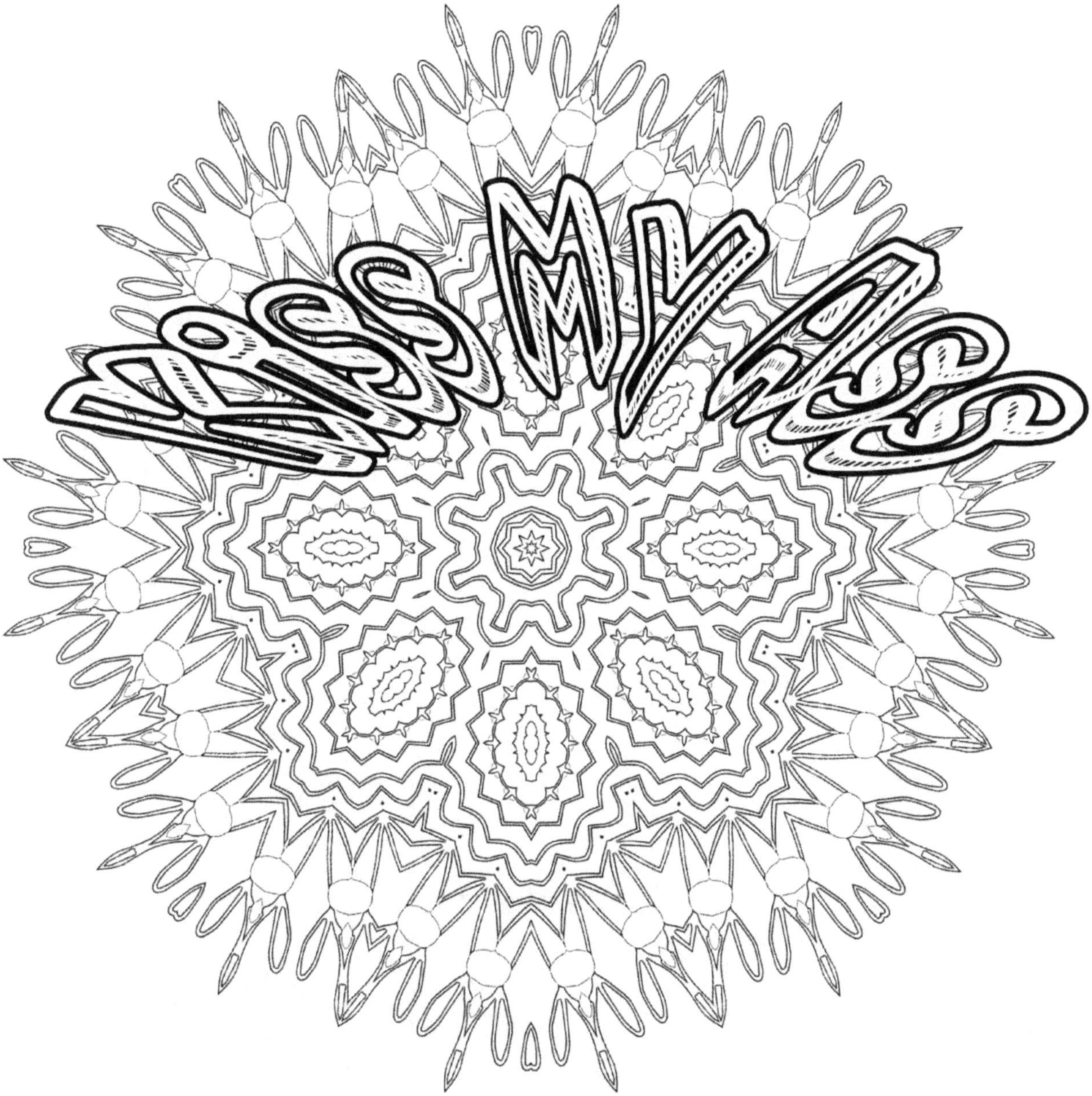
KISS MY ASS

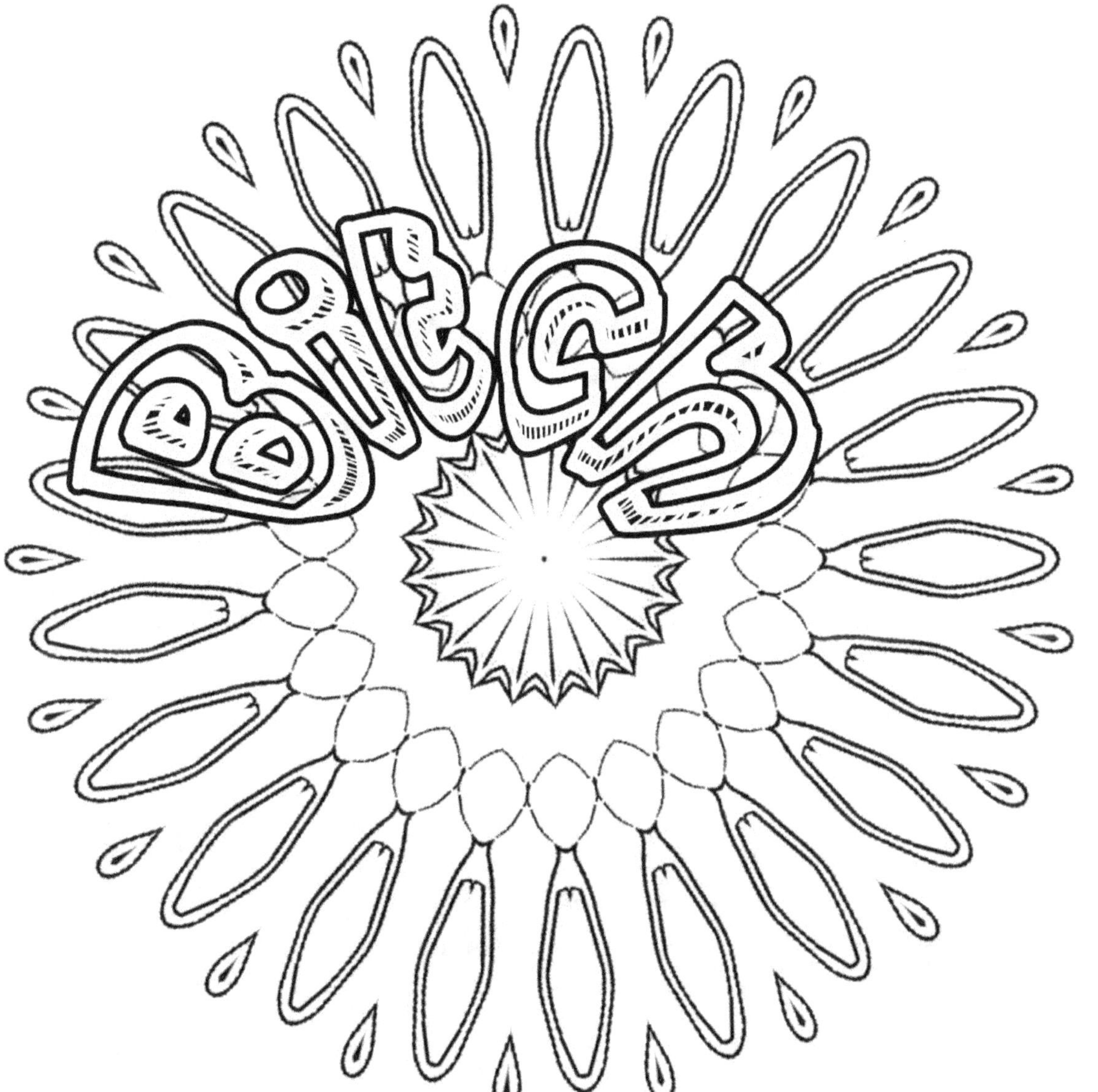
Bitch

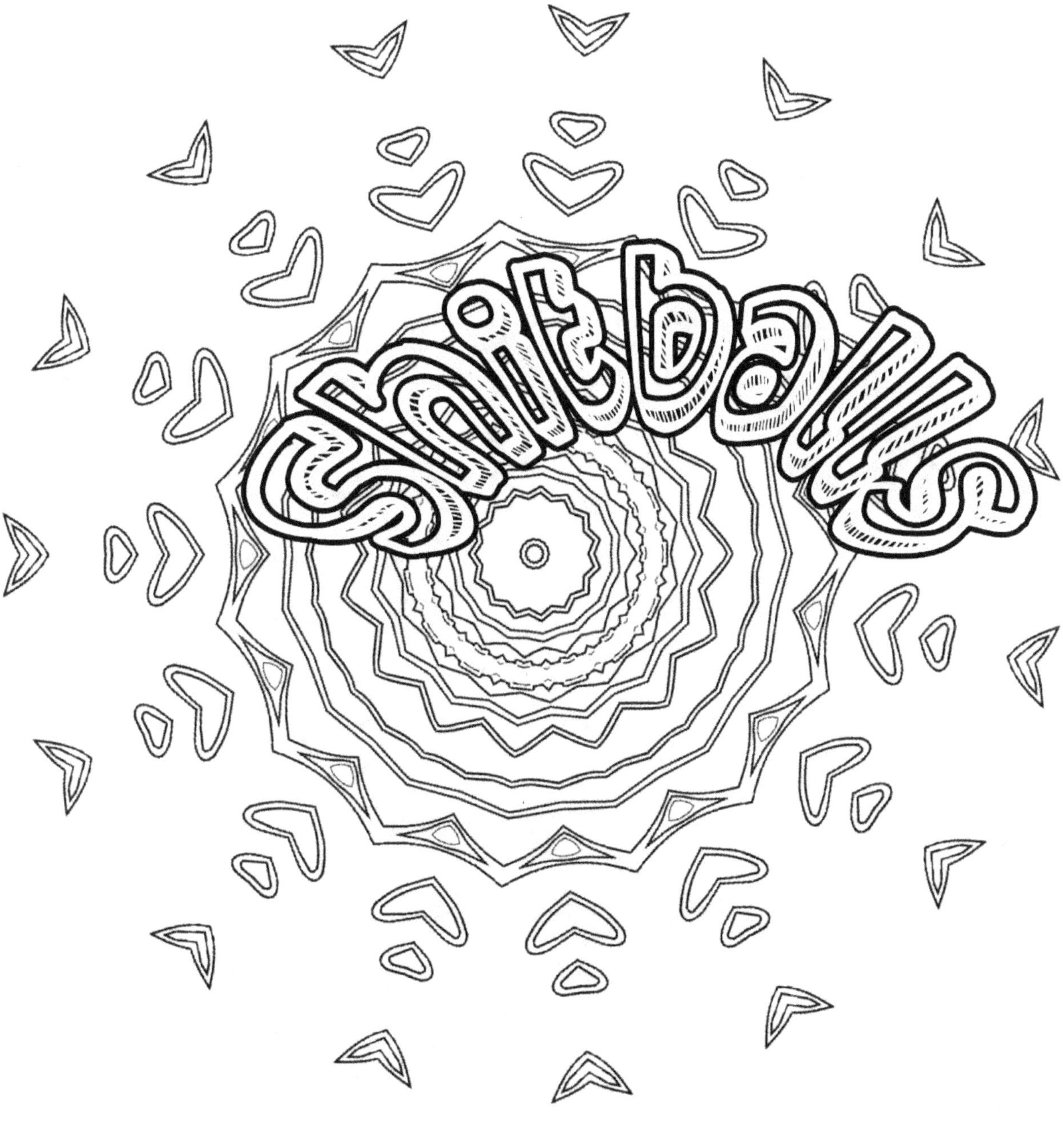
shitballs

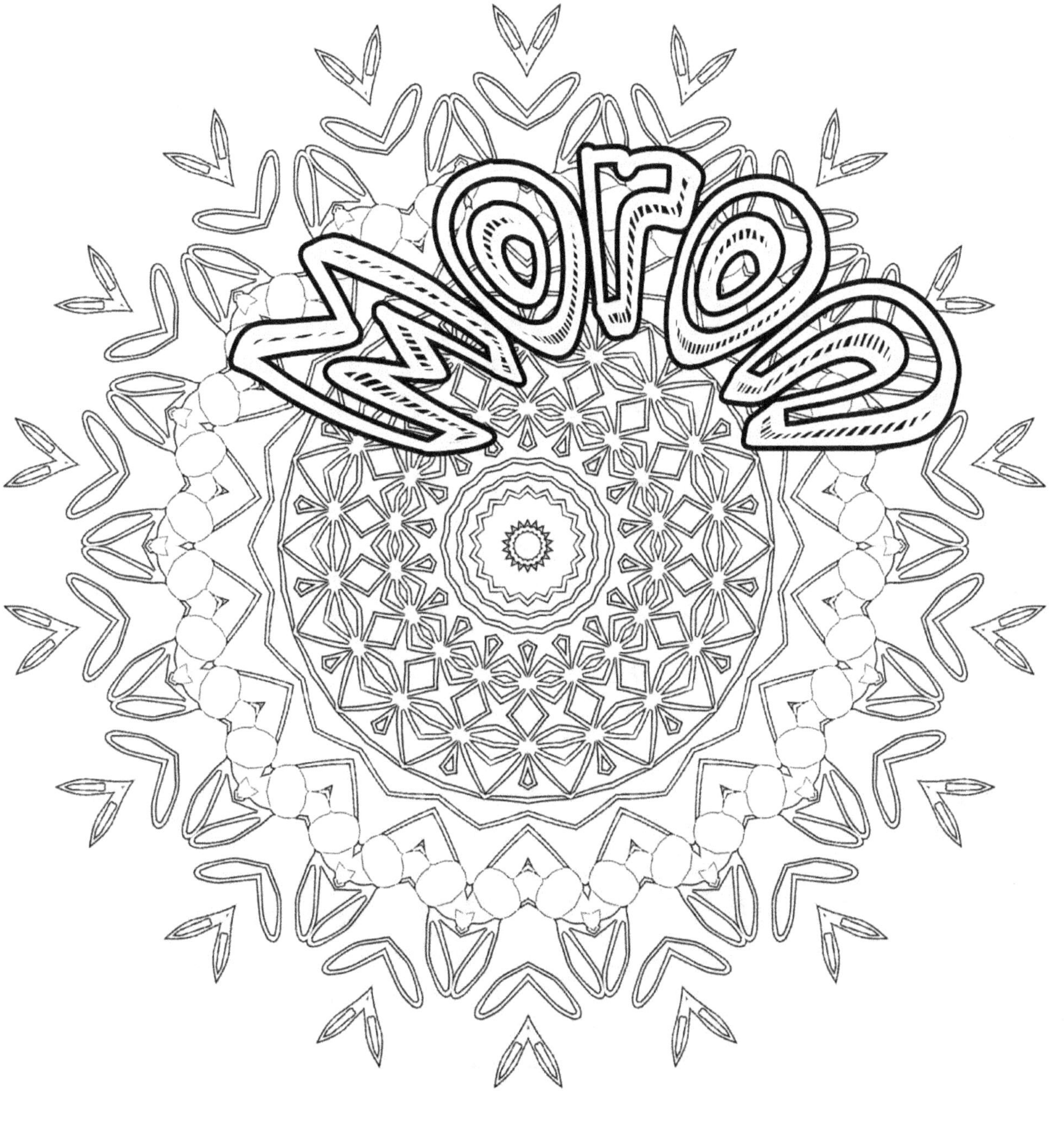
moron

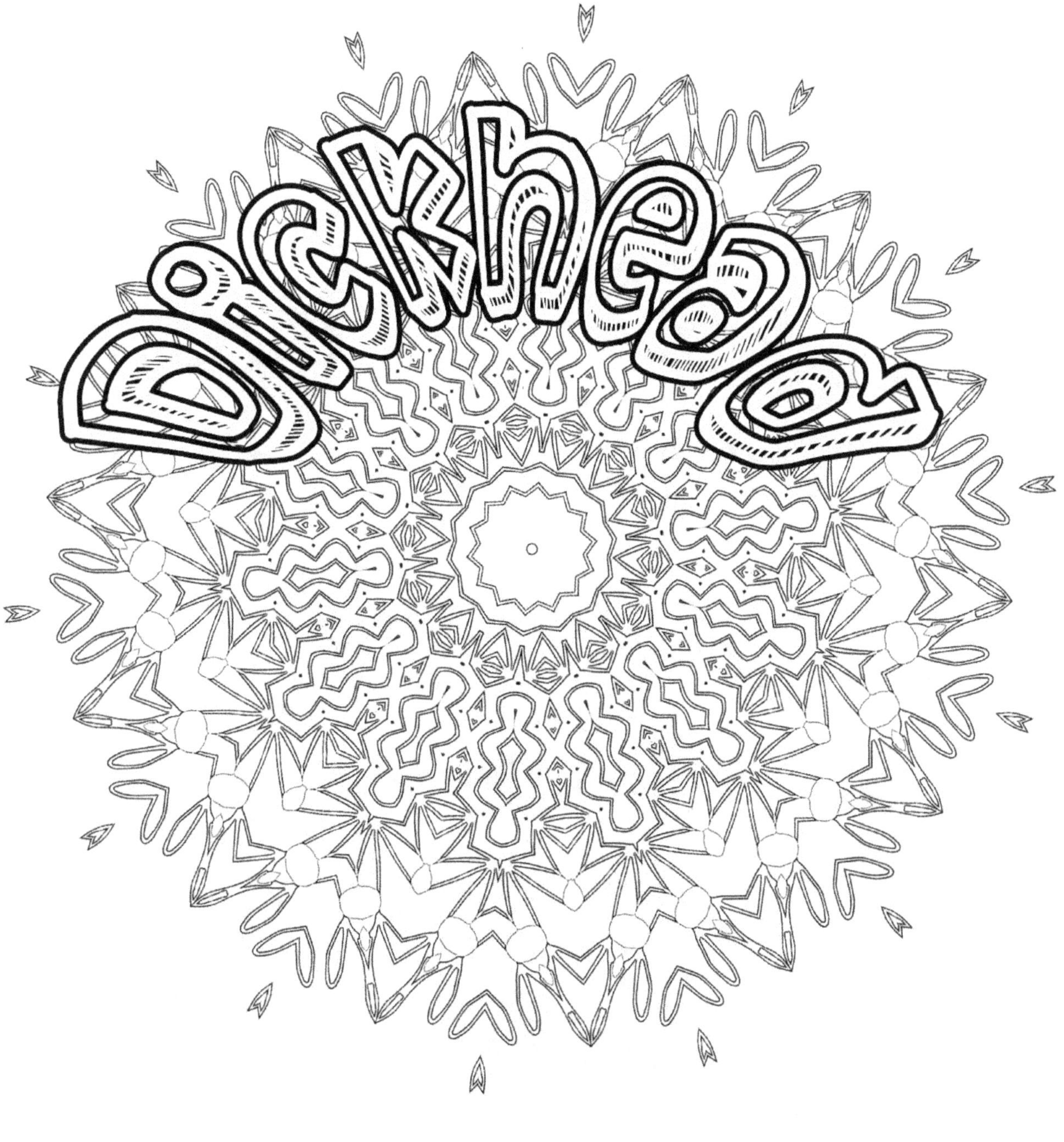
Dickhead

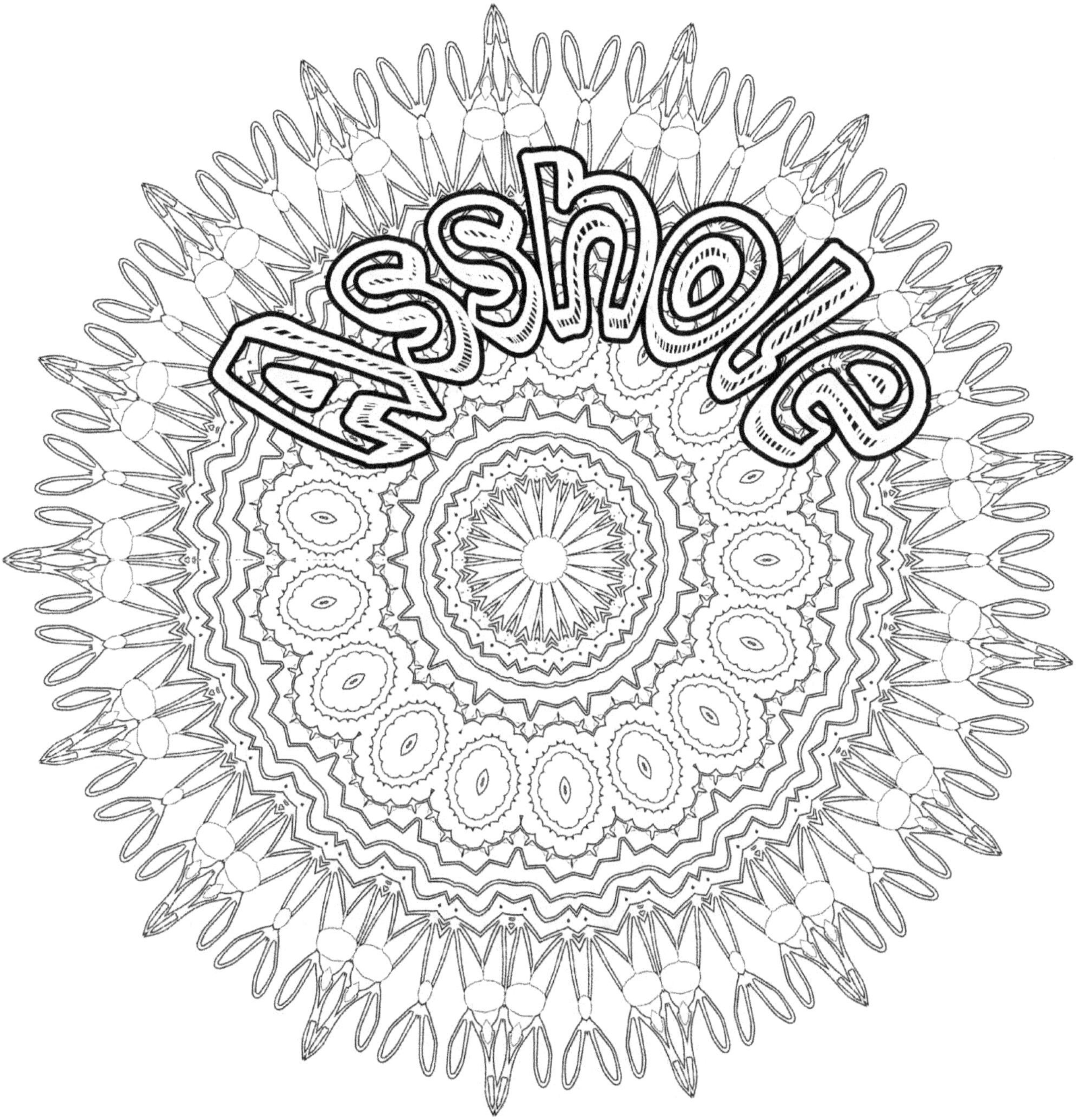
Asshole

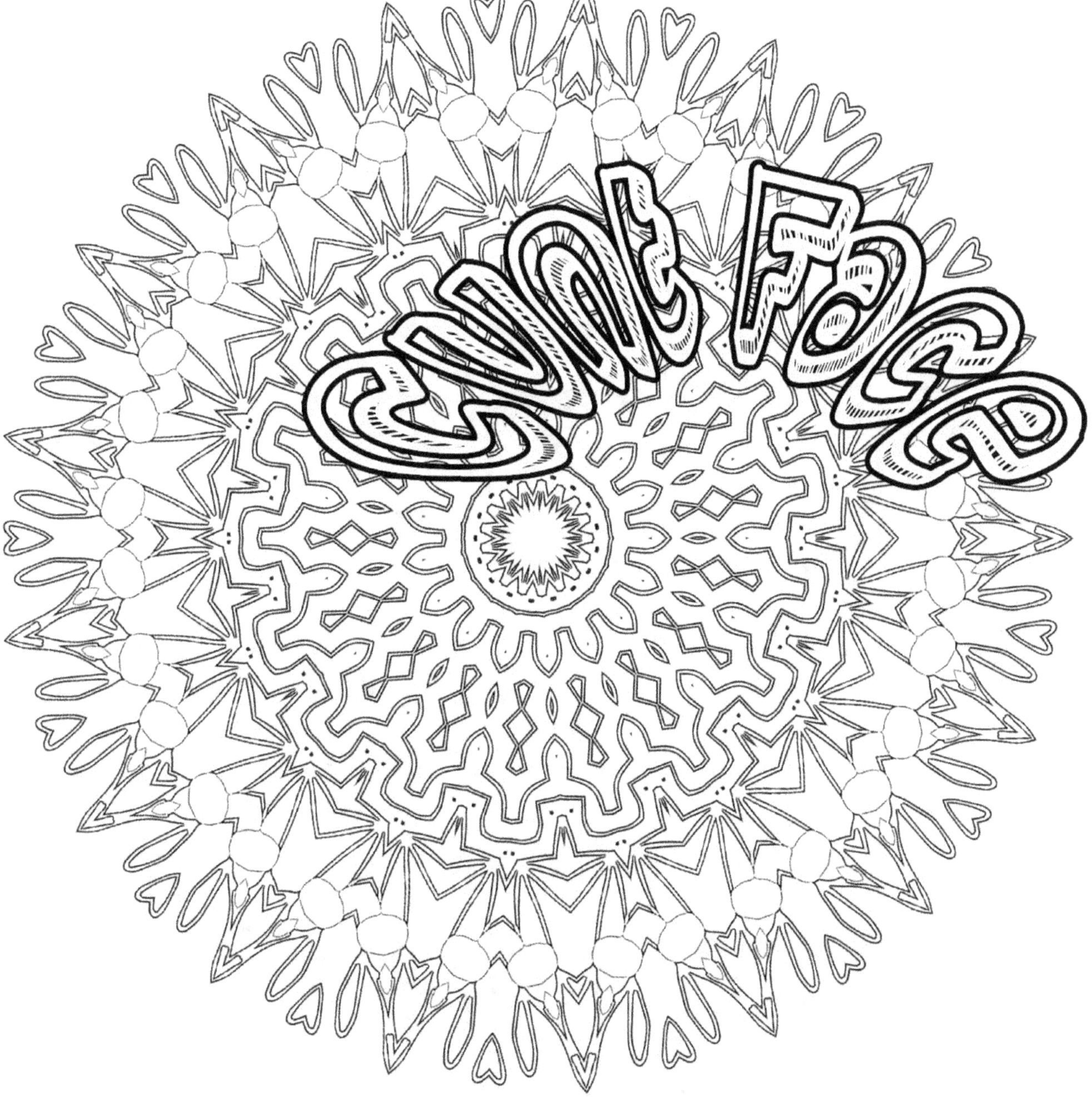
Cunt Face

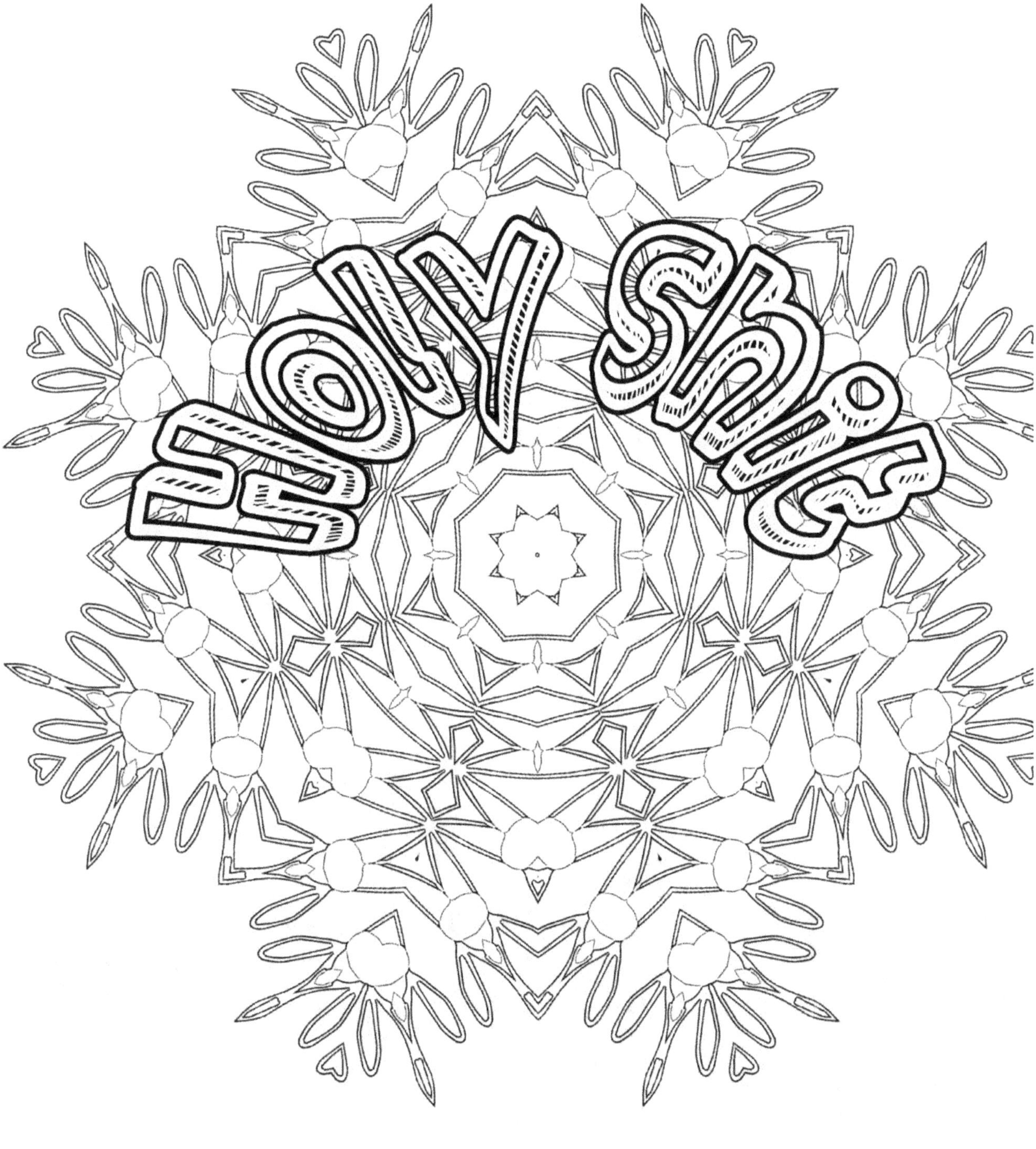
Holy Shit

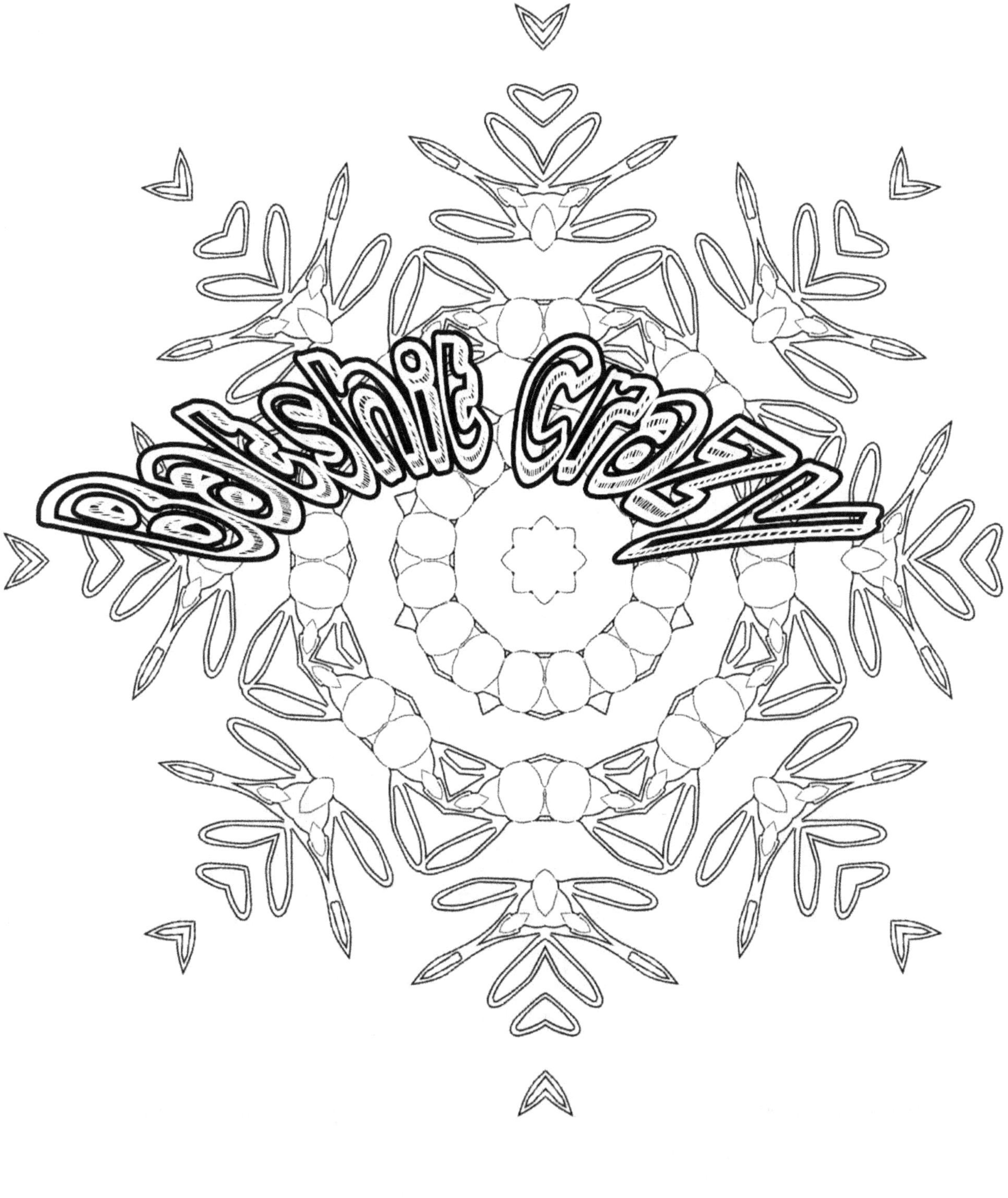
Batshit Crazy

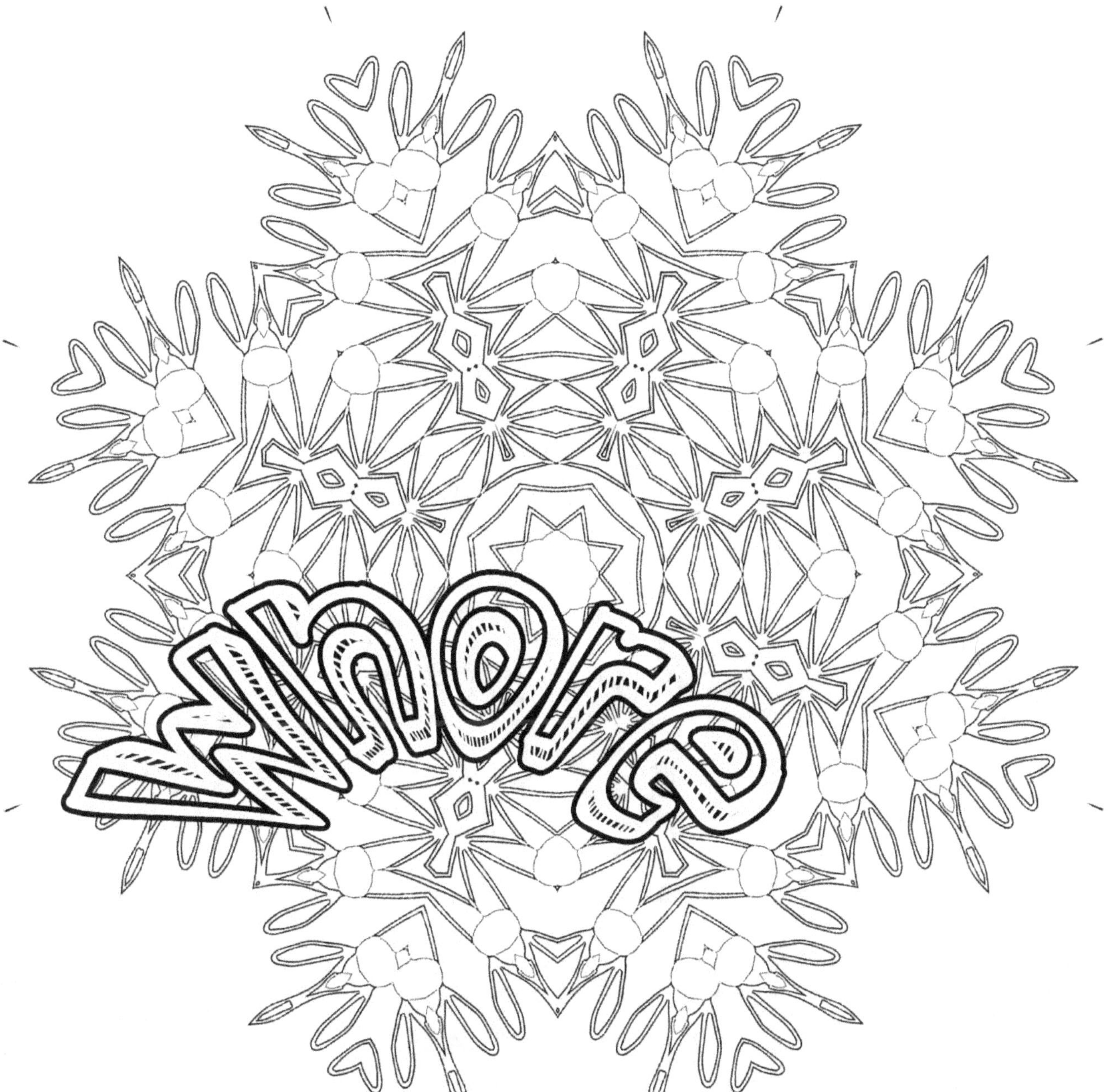
whore

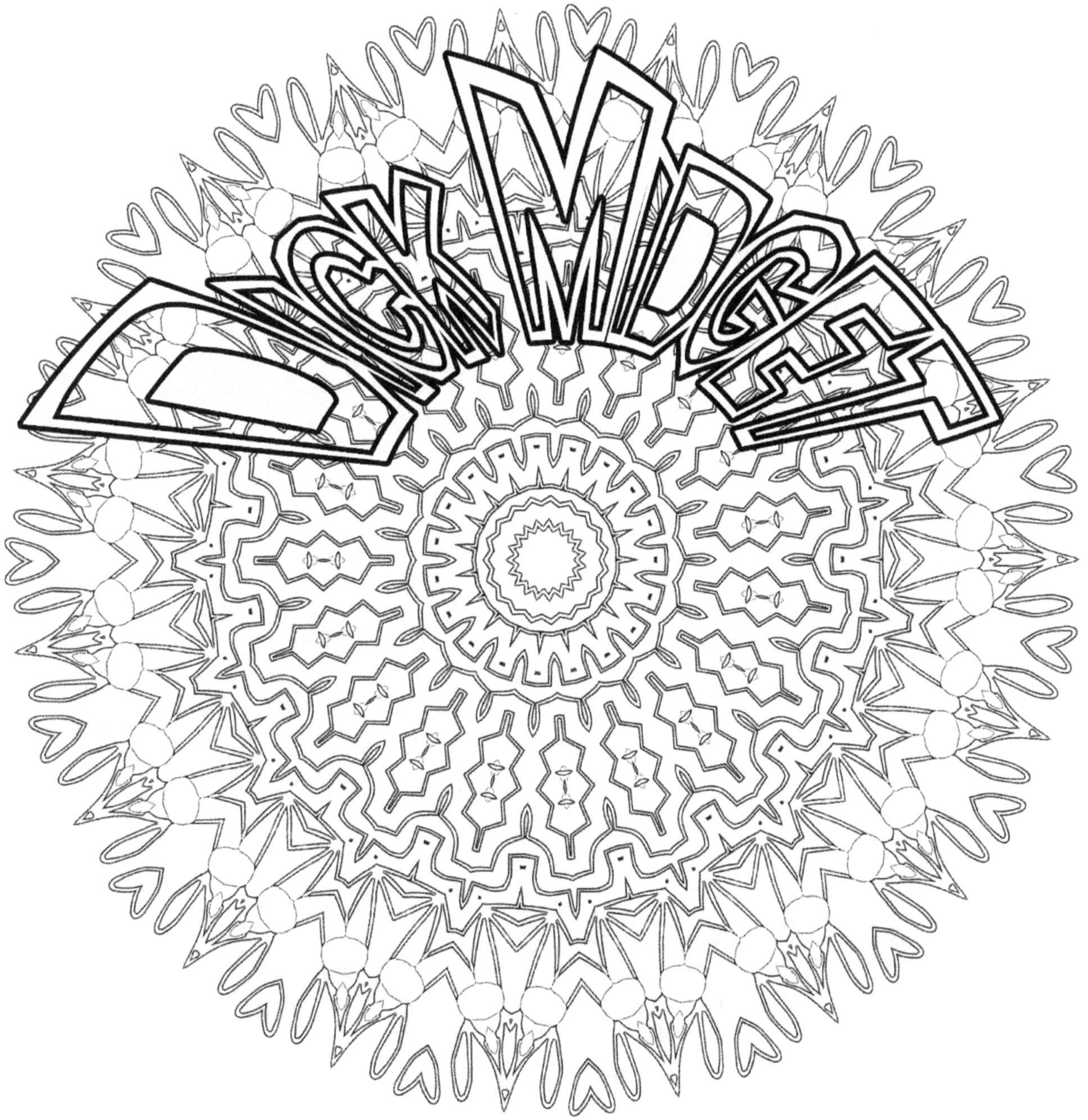

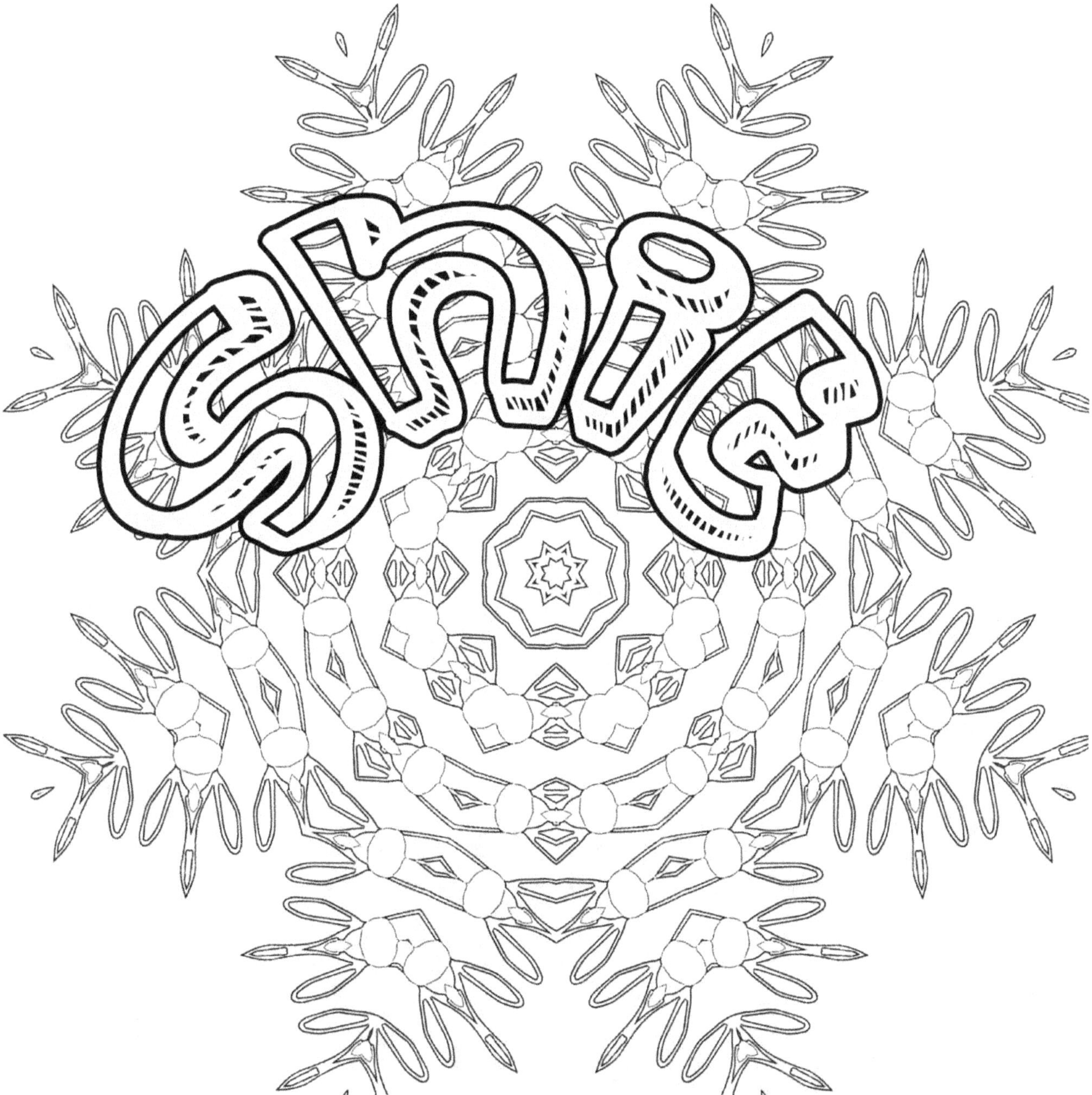
Chic

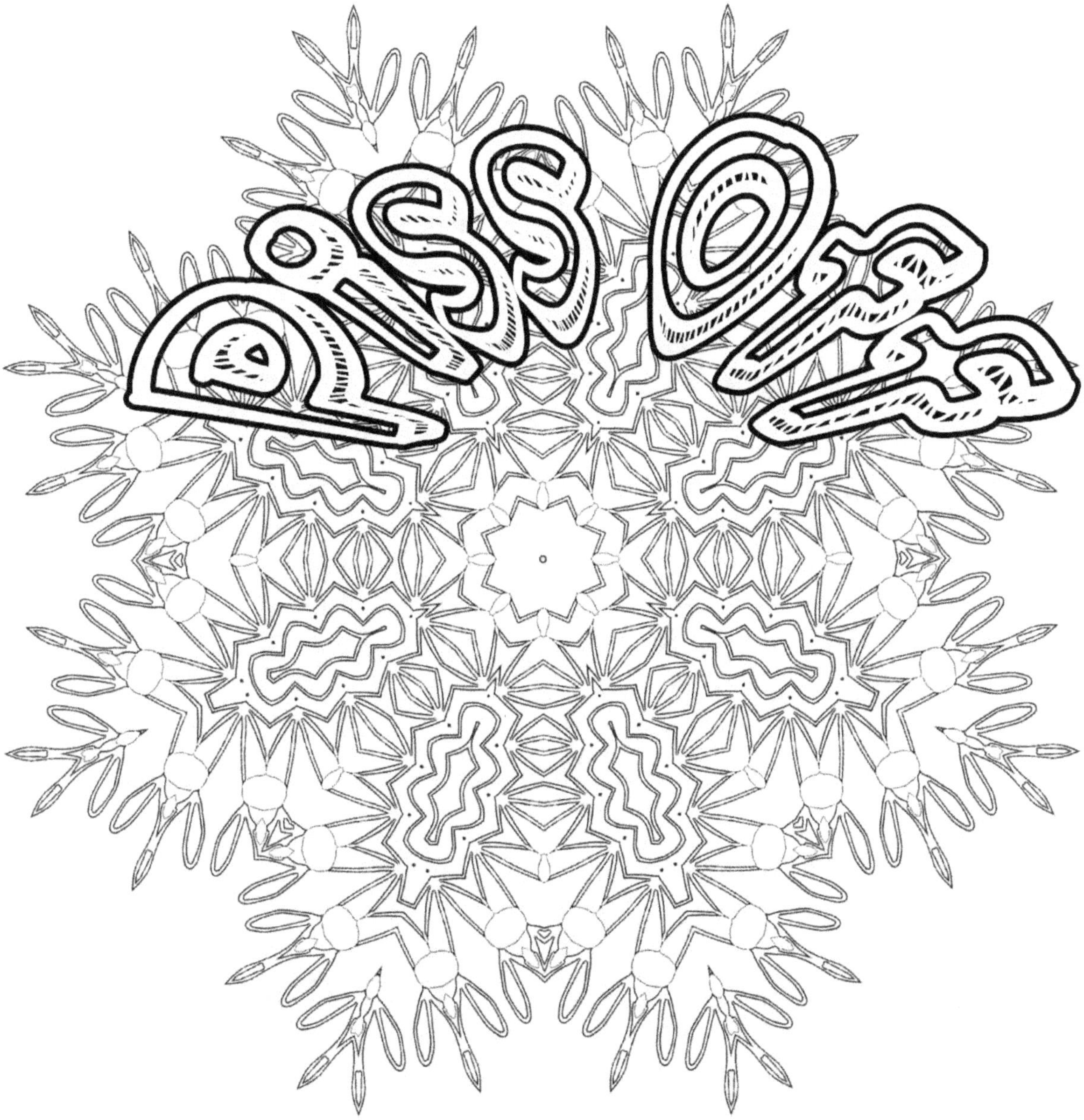
Dissolve

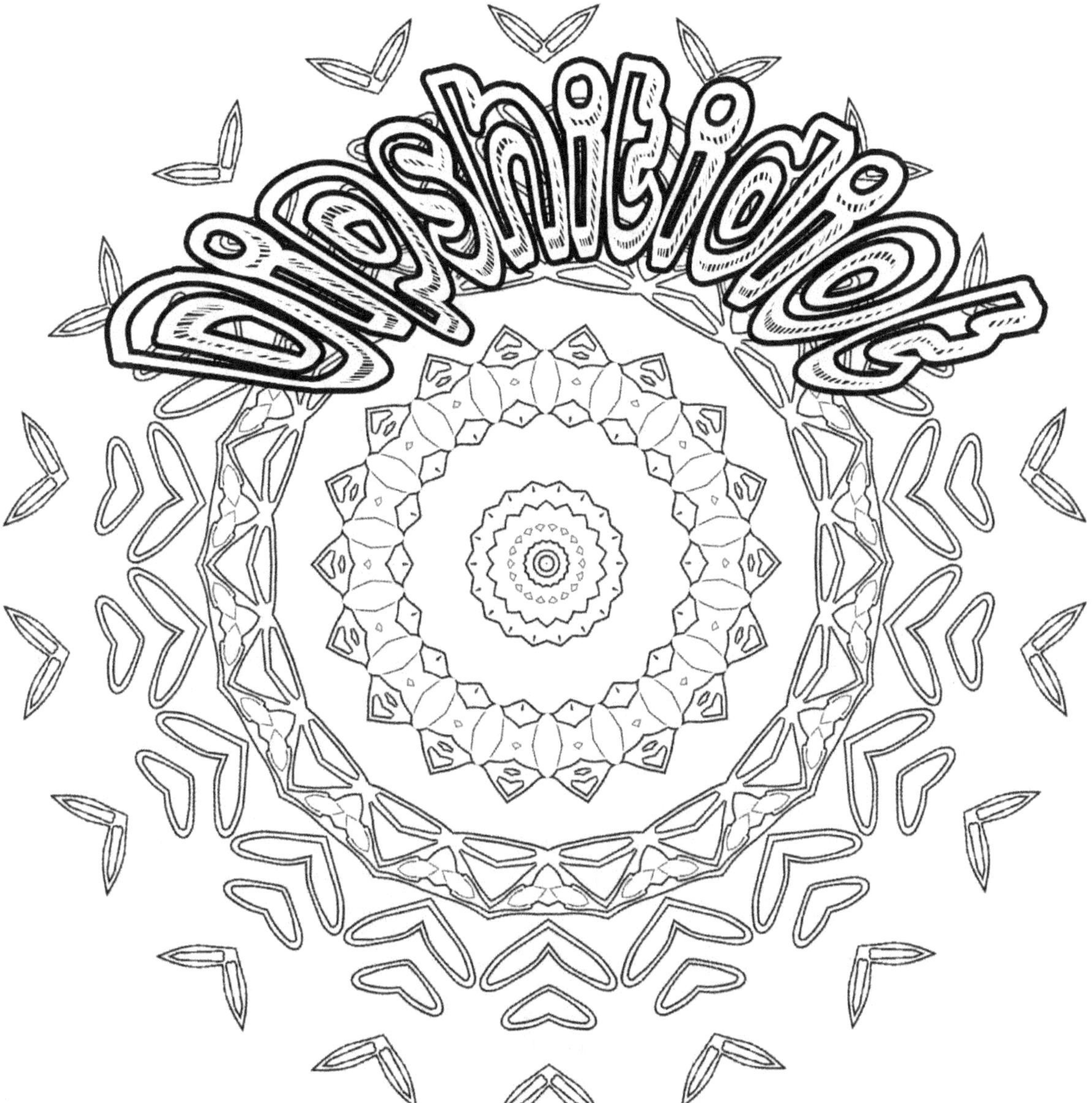
Dipshitidiots

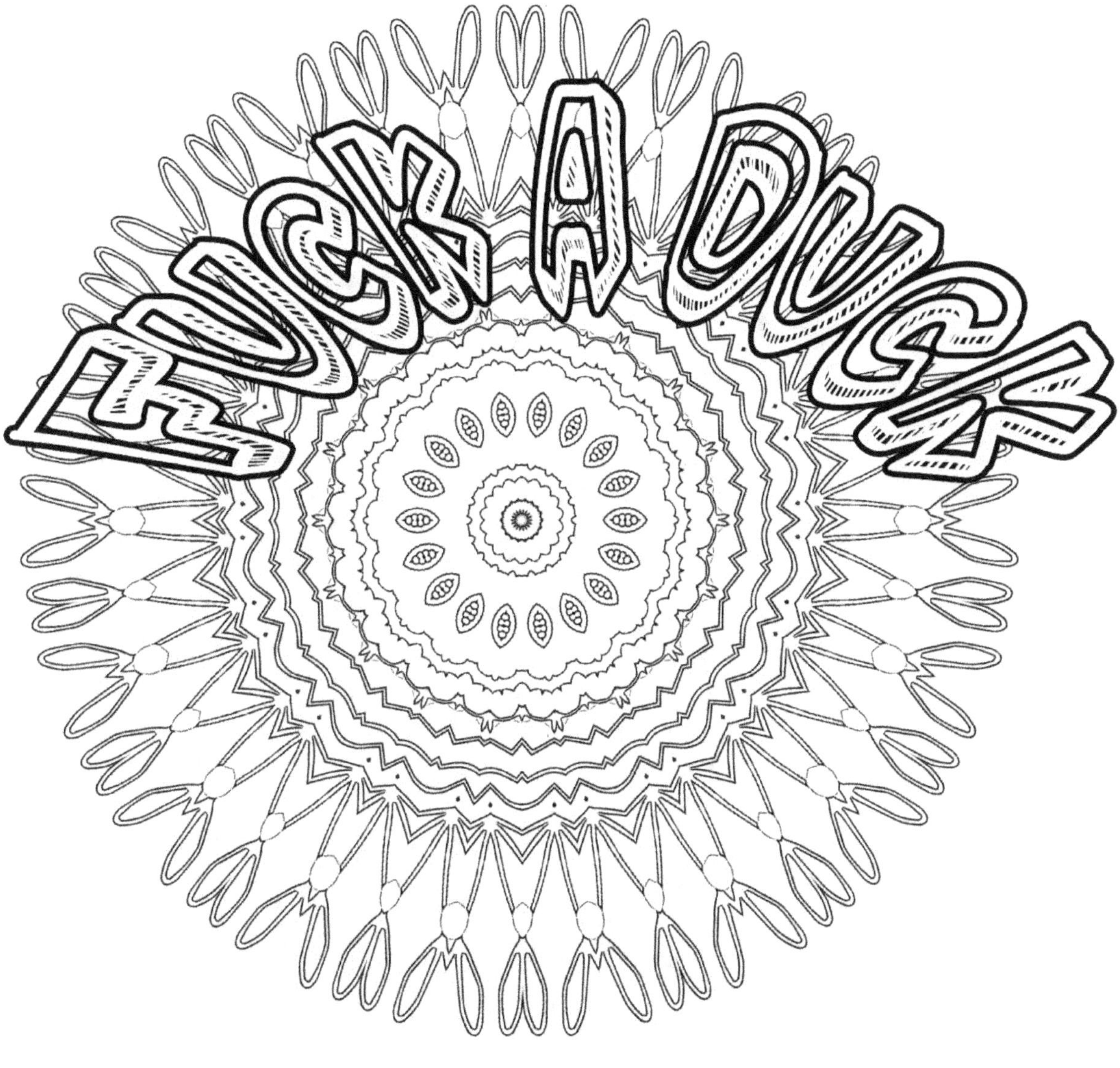
FUCK A DUCK

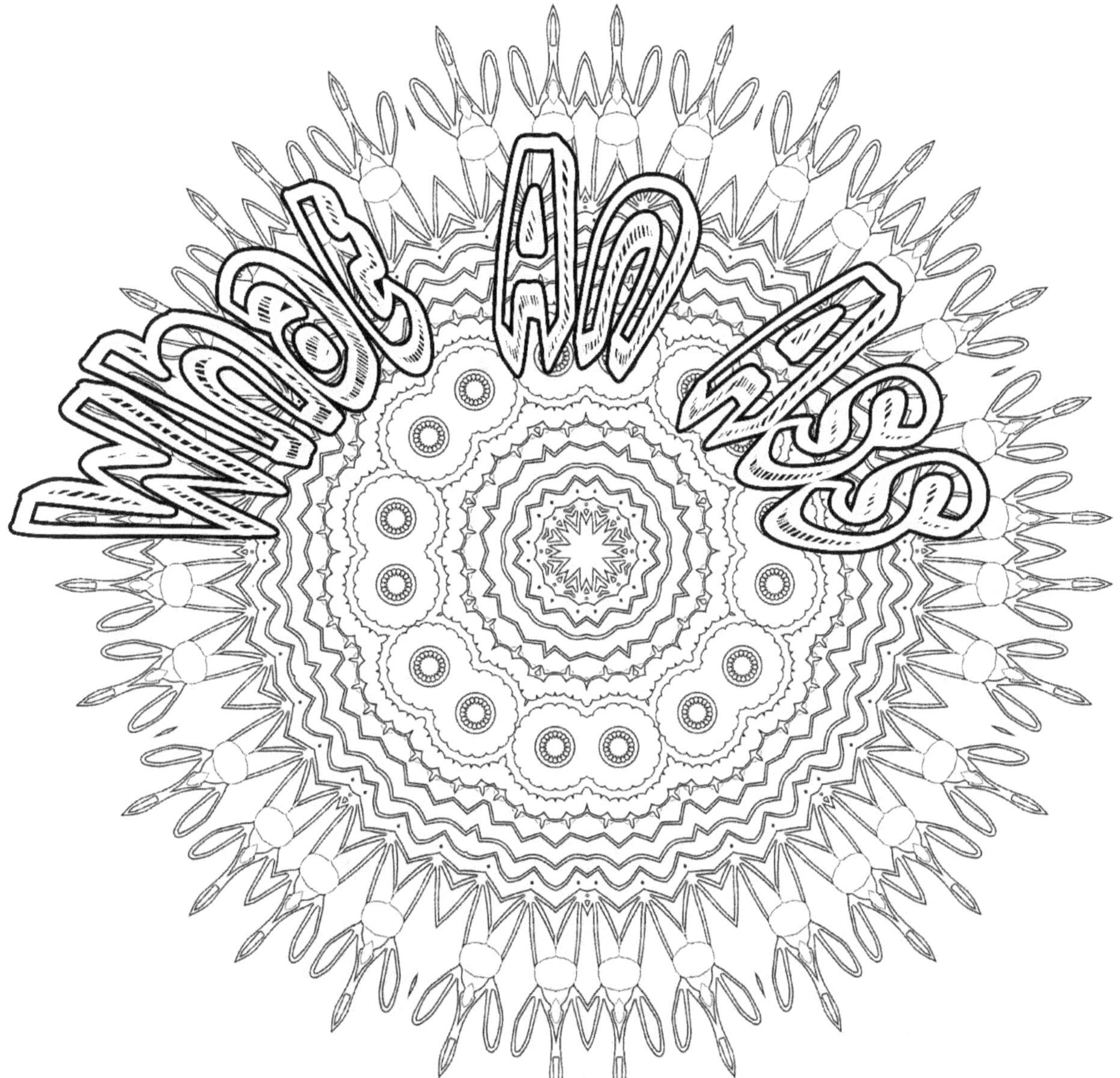
What An Ass

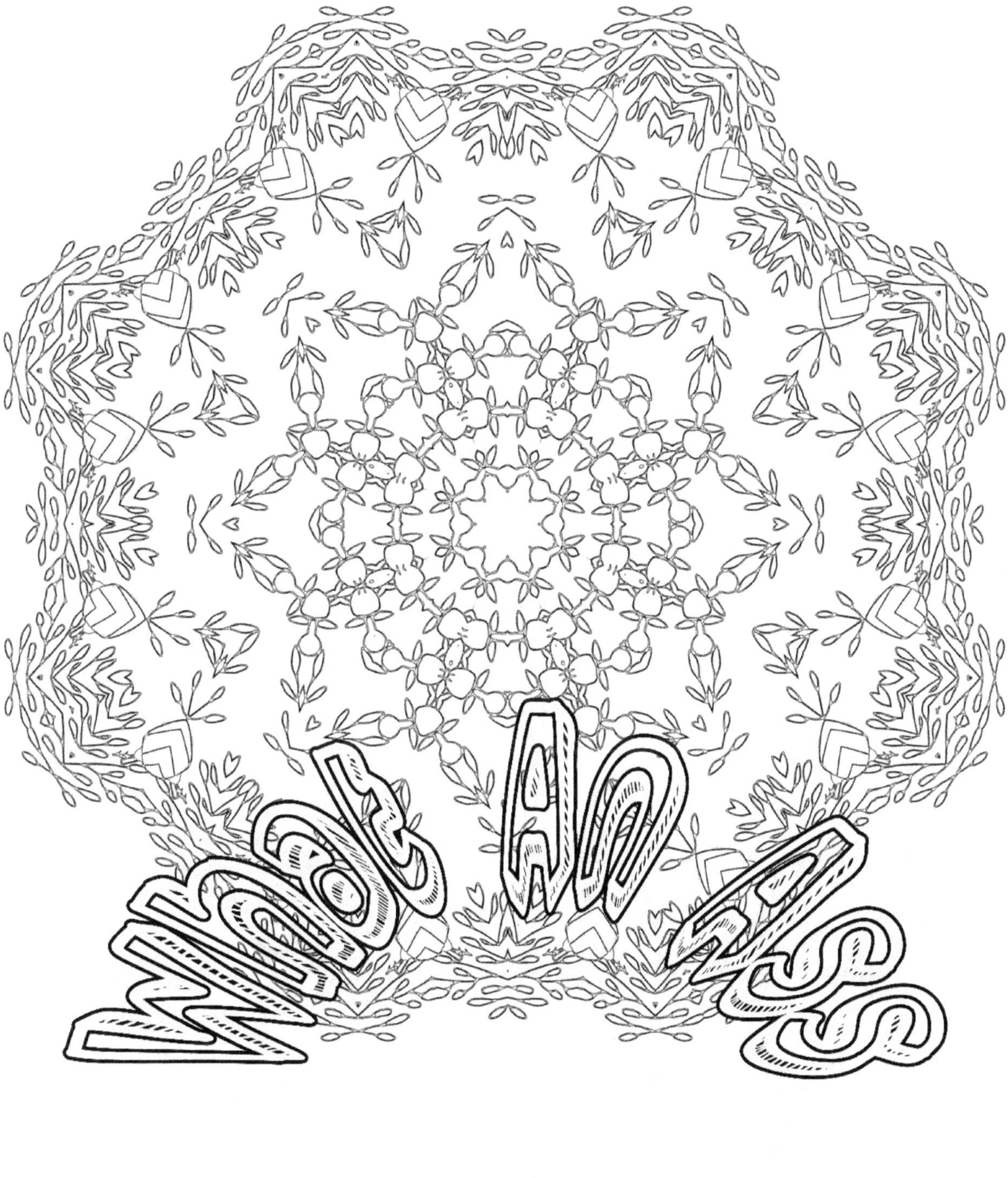
What An Ass

www.ingramcontent.com/pod-product-compliance
Lightning Source LLC
Chambersburg PA
CBHW081749170526
45167CB00009B/3981
* 9 7 8 1 5 4 4 1 8 1 0 1 1 *